How t
with Grief, Loss, and Death

A Survivor's Guide to Coping with Pain and Trauma, and Learning to Live Again

Richard Banks

Introduction

Congratulations on purchasing *How to Deal with Loss, Grief, and Death,* and thank you for doing so.

At some point in our lives, we have to face one harsh reality. The realization of our own mortality and the genuine possibility that we will one day lose the people we love, sometimes sooner than we think. Although somewhere deep inside ourselves, we understand that this very precious life that we live must come to an end one day, we can never truly be prepared for losing the people that we love.

Everyone goes through the grieving process in their own way, and there is no universal method for healing. Your grieving process is going to be as unique as you are. However, the one thing that we all share is the fact that we will never be ready for that fateful day. We will never be prepared to lose the people we love, and when it happens, the pain and shock of the loss can hit you so hard it can feel like you will never be fine again.

Everyone struggles to cope with losing the ones that they love. How do you ever prepare to say goodbye to those whom you love *so much* and those that you could never imagine your life without? What can you do to process that pain in the most healthy way possible without jeopardizing your health and wellbeing in your devastated state? Therein lies the problem. Grief and loss are such a harrowing experience, and the healing process sometimes feels impossible. It might feel as though this lingering pain will stay with you forever, and you have no idea how to help yourself, let alone help anyone else who may be dependent on you during this challenging time.

There is no quick fix to the problem. There is no magic formula, no special pill or potion you can take that will numb the pain and make you feel better about this terrible loss in your life. When you lose the people you love, it inevitably leaves a large, gaping hole in your life where their presence once was. That is why I have chosen to write this book to help you work through your grief. You see, grief is not a process that can be rushed. It is a very painful and emotional journey, and it is not something you can fix by merely watching a YouTube video or two. It is not going to be that simple, unfortunately, but every step you are going to read about in this book is designed to help you understand what you are going through. As you peruse the next few chapters of this book and go through the steps, understand that you are not alone in this process. It can feel that way because you are at one of the lowest points in your life, but you *can* find strength in this time of darkness if you have the right coping mechanisms and support by your side.

Grief is always a painful process to deal with, but I can promise you the techniques, and coping mechanisms in this book have been written to help you feel a little more comfortable with the uncomfortable. This book will be your guide for when you're not ready to open up to anyone else just yet about your loss. No one should ever be alone during the most painful times in their lives, and hopefully, this book will help you feel like you are not alone. Other friends and family members are going to try and help you in the best way they know-how. Admittedly, they might utter unhelpful phrases like "be strong" or "move on." They don't mean to be hurtful. They are simply trying to help in the only way that they know. But you don't have to "move on" from your grief because you will never truly move on. The people you love that you have lost will be a part of your life forever. You won't be the only person that slips easily into the present tense when you talk about them because the ones you have lost will always have a special presence in your life. You will still feel their presence, even if they are not physically around anymore. It doesn't make you weird or strange, and it doesn't mean you're in denial or not coping with that loss because you're not "moving on" the way other people think you should. There is no such thing as moving on from a loved one who has had a very special place in your life.

Everything you are about to learn in this book is designed to help you learn how to live your life after your loved one's passing. The day you get the news of their passing is an unthinkable one, but picking up the pieces of your life is possible. When it comes to dealing with grief and loss, you never really move on. Instead, you move forward. Your loved one will always be a part of your life in some way, as long as you remember them and think about them. They will be with you for the rest of your life, and there will be times when you feel their presence strongly. They're not going to be present in the same way they were before, but they will be present in your life. This new way of living without them is something you can learn how to manage with time, and this is why you're here right now reading this book. When someone you love dies, there is no such thing as moving on, but there is such a thing called living again because that is what the resilient human spirit is meant to do. We grow stronger with every experience, and if you are ready to find out how to live your life again and rise from this painful time, let's begin.

There are plenty of books on this subject on the market, thanks again for choosing this one! Every effort was made to ensure it is full of as much useful information as possible. Please enjoy!

CHAPTER 1: WHAT IS GRIEF?

The pain of losing someone we love cannot be described in words. It feels like your whole world is falling apart. The crushing pain in your chest is indicative of your heart breaking into a million pieces. It feels like the tears will never stop flowing. Your whole world has been turned upside down, and you might even feel like you will never smile again. It is never easy to have a loved one pass away, even if their death is an expected one. Knowing that you will never see the one you love again and knowing that you will have to live out the rest of your life without them is a crushing feeling. It can feel like a burden that is too much to bear, and it is normal to feel like you are never going to survive this sadness. Grief is not limited to human loved ones alone. Many people feel this same sense of despair when a pet who was a beloved member of the family passes away.

What Is Grief?

Grief is a reaction that happens when someone we love or care about deeply dies. When this happens, a whole host of emotions might overwhelm you. Some of these emotions include feeling sad, angry, confused, or scared. Sometimes these emotions come one at a time, and sometimes they could happen altogether. Grief could even make you feel physically sick, where you have trouble eating, sleeping, or sometimes breathing. No matter what you are going through, it is okay to feel the way you do. You are never alone, and you are not wrong.

The sudden and shocking death of a loved one is perhaps the most challenging form of grief to overcome because it happened completely out of the blue. You had no time to prepare for it, and the news is a complete shock to your system. It is absolutely devastating to lose someone you love, and there is nothing anyone can say or do at that moment that will make you feel better.

After someone dies, some people might feel the need to be alone. They avoid contact with the outside world and even turn away from their friends and family. Some people process grief in a different way. They don't want to be alone during this difficult time and might actively seek out the company of trusted friends and family members.

Everyone processes grief differently. Some people might find that they are easily distracted for several weeks, perhaps even crying on and off throughout the day. Some people might even try to hide their grief to avoid making the people around them uncomfortable, but this is not a healthy way to process all the emotions you feel. Whatever emotions you feel, it is completely normal. You need to acknowledge that loss as a part of your recovery process. You could be feeling numb, or perhaps you feel nothing at all. Some people feel completely shattered, unable to function for weeks in their regular routine. Some people become mute for several weeks as a part of how they grieve.

There is a range of ways different people could cope with the emotions that they go through, and the grieving process is not going to be the same for everyone. Regardless of how you feel, it is essential to acknowledge that this is all part of how you process this difficult moment in your life.

At some stages during your grieving, you might feel guilty. Some part of you might think that you are to blame for the person's death somehow. Perhaps it was something you said or thought about the deceased that triggers this feeling within you. You will think about and recall many moments you had with your loved ones when they pass, and some of those memories are going to make you cry, while others may make you feel guilty. It is important to understand that you are not to be blamed in any way. *It is not your fault that your loved one died,* no matter how your emotions might try to convince you otherwise. Grief is chaotic, messy, and unpredictable. Nothing about the process is something you can prepare for.

Grief is an ongoing process. Even when you think you are fine, sometimes a memory, place, sight, sound, or smell might trigger a wave of emotions all over again. This can happen even years or decades after a person has passed away. This grieving process can also occur when you have lost a beloved pet who was like a family member to you. Years after your pet's passing, a photograph, a memory, or even the anniversary of your pet's death, can bring back those painful emotions all over again. These waves of emotion that you feel are completely normal, and it will fade away after a while.

This is a process that is extremely personal and unique. There is no specific way to grieve, and everyone has to find their own way to work through the process. At the same time, the process of grieving is a paradox, one where you have to find a way of living with the reality of your loss. Pain is going to be the agent of change in this process. This pain will be the agent that forces you to adjust to this new reality. Pain is something nobody ever wants to deal with. From an early age, we have developed defenses and coping mechanisms to protect us against this pain. Coping mechanisms could include alcohol, working longer hours than you should, gambling, smoking, sex, avoidance, destructive relationships, and more. However, your avoidance of this pain will eventually do more harm than good.

How Grief Affects Us

There are five to seven stages of grief that we typically go through; however, not everyone goes through all seven stages. Everyone experiences grief differently. Some people might only experience five stages, whereas others might go through all seven. The stages of grief are:

- **Stage One -** Shock
- **Stage Two -** Denial
- **Stage Three -** Pain
- **Stage Four -** Anger
- **Stage Five -** Bargaining
- **Stage Six -** Depression

- **Stage Seven -** Acceptance

Since every individual is unique, it comes as no surprise that we would go through these stages in very different ways. For example, you and your sibling might have lost the same loved one, but the two of you would go through the stages of grief in a way that is unique to you. It's natural to have high and low moments during this process.

While you are grieving, others might sprout out common phrases for those faced with such a difficult situation. They might tell you something along the lines of *hang in there, everything will be alright in the end, stay strong,* or *it will get better eventually*. They mean well, but a grieving person rarely finds such statements helpful. These statements may not always be true, but they are only trying to comfort you in the best way they know-how. It is hard to figure out what to say to a person who has experienced such a heartbreaking loss.

There are other aspects involved in the grieving process that no one ever tells you about. Grieving has a very painful way of affecting you in ways you probably never even imagined.

- **You Grieve for More Than Just the Deceased Person -** Their loss saddens you, but you are grieving for more than just the deceased. Their death is the most common source of your grief, but you are affected by this loss in such an intense way because *it is not* the only thing you are grieving. You grieve for the time you will never get to spend with them. You grieve for all the things you planned to do together but can't. You grieve for the absence of this person in your life. You grieve for all the things you wished you could have done before you lost them. You grieve for the life that you have ahead of you without them in it. You grieve for the loss of the relationship and the love that you once had.

- **Staying Strong is Not as Easy as It Seems -** Staying strong is not as easy as it seems when it feels like your heart is breaking into a million pieces. Staying strong only happens *after* you have gone through the grief process properly. Don't blame yourself if you find it a struggle to stay strong during this challenging time, even though several people around you have encouraged you to do it. You don't have to do anything until you've experienced the grieving process in its entirety. Perhaps instead of saying "be strong," we would be much better off if people told us that it was alright *not* to be strong while we grieve. It is OK to cry, scream, take some time off for yourself, and it is OK to feel like you don't have the strength to go through the day. You don't have to force yourself to do anything that you are not ready for. If you push yourself too hard, you might make the grieving process even harder on yourself than it normally would be.

- **Grief Will Make You Question Certain Things -** Not everyone will experience this, but for some people, this is one way that grief affects them. It makes them question certain things, like why this tragedy had to happen. Feelings of guilt and regret are normal. You might feel like you could have done or said something that might have prevented the tragedy. Feeling a sense of guilt is not unhealthy, and it is a normal part of the grieving process. However, it does become unhealthy if you don't learn to let this guilt go eventually. There is nothing for you to gain by choosing to hold on to this guilt. It won't change what has happened, no matter how many times you choose to blame yourself for it.

- **Not All Wounds Are Going to Heal -** Time will not necessarily heal all wounds. It merely soothes them over and makes it easier for you to go through the day. The days will start to feel easier eventually, but the wound may never fully be healed, depending on the relationship you had with the person. This is OK. Some scars will never truly fade. It is normal to be haunted by the loss and still grieve, even years after the loved one's passing. You don't have to be down on yourself for being emotionally caught up in the past sometimes. Trauma and tragedy will never completely go away.

The Seven Stages of Grief Explained

From the moment we find out that someone we love dies, the stages of grief begin to kick in. Again, this will be exhibited differently depending on the individual. Not everyone will go through all seven phases, and it is possible to go through two phases simultaneously. Understanding the stages of grief will help you work through your emotions and cope with your loss better when you know what you are dealing with. It will also prepare you for what you can expect when the next stage rolls around. More importantly, it will help you better work through any feelings of guilt or regret that you may have trouble releasing.

Some people might find themselves stuck at certain stages of the grieving process. When this happens, it is crucial to understand that grief will always involve some amount of pain. The pain is something you cannot avoid, even though you try your best to do it. To fully recover from your tragedy, the pain is something you will have to work through, even though this is admittedly going to be very difficult.

- **Stage One: Shock -** Shock is the first reaction that most people have, especially if the death occurred suddenly. Nothing can ever truly prepare you for the news of the devastating loss. When you receive the news of a loved one's passing, your body goes into shock mode. You feel numb and unable to process anything, and it feels like you can't move at times. Numbness is your body's way of only allowing you to deal with the emotions you are capable of handling at that time.

- **Stage Two: Denial -** This will be quickly accompanied by the intense pain that you try so hard to avoid. Denial happens because you're still in disbelief at the sudden absence of this person. Depending on how close they were to you, they could have left a gaping hole in your life, an empty void that you have no idea how to fill. Shock and denial are one of the two stages of grief that can happen simultaneously. Denial happens because your mind cannot process the horror of this loss, and this is your mind's way of protecting you from the pain that is about to wash over you. Some people refuse to accept the news of the death and may even choose to believe that someone they know might be pulling a practical joke on them. Denial can be a temporarily helpful stage of the grieving process to avoid overwhelming you all at once. However, you will need to accept reality at some point, and this includes accepting the next range of painful emotions that will follow. Should you find yourself stuck in this stage, you will need some help. This help can come from a close friend, a relative, a trained therapist, or a grief counselor.

- **Stage Three: Pain -** Once you emerge from the denial phase, the next stage is pain. This stage is going to hit you with its full blast. It is going to be very crushing and overwhelming. Unfortunately, some people will find it very tempting at this stage to numb the pain with alcohol or drugs. However, it is essential to remember that this is a necessary stage of the grieving process. It may not seem like it, but the pain is healing you. It heals you and prepares you to work through your guilt. The excruciating pain you go through could lead to anxiety and depression, which is another stage in this process. The pain is going to be part of your life throughout the grieving process and beyond.

- **Stage Four: Anger** - Once you work through the intense pain, you might experience feelings of anger. The pain can be overwhelming, and that pain can lead to very powerful feelings of anger. This anger could be directed toward the doctors who couldn't do anything else to save the life of your loved one. Anger could be directed toward the friends or relatives whom you thought should have been there for you. You might even feel angry with God for taking away this loved one from your life when you were not ready to lose them just yet. The truth is, you will never be prepared to lose the people that you love. You might ask questions like why you have to go through this instead of someone else. Anger can be another helpful stage of the grieving process because it gives you some sense of control. After the previous stage, where all you felt was overwhelming pain, anger gives you some sense of control again. It can be a beneficial outlet for your devastating pain, as long as you remember not to vent this anger out at the people you love. They are grieving too, and they are in just as much pain as you are. Anger is a stage that can last for days, weeks, or months, and it is vital during this stage that you keep an eye out for signs of uncontrolled anger. This could be a sign that you need help.

- **Stage Five: Bargaining -** This stage can accompany any of the other previous four stages mentioned above. For example, when you are feeling intense pain or guilt, you might resort to bargaining. You might try bargaining with God, promising to be a better person if only he would save the life of your loved one. Bargaining is a stage that can be particularly powerful when you have a loved one who has been diagnosed with a terminal illness of some sort. Bargaining for the life of your loved one offers some kind of hope or a channel for your pain. Bargaining is a stage that doesn't happen to everyone, and it would depend on the circumstances of the loss.

- **Stage Six: Depression** – Depression, and loneliness is the next stage that follows. This is the point in your grieving process where you feel the loss of your loved one the most, especially if you lived with them. The reality that you have to now live out the rest of your days without them is *devastating,* and it can quickly lead to depression and feelings of loneliness. Depression follows when you finally realize that your loved one is gone and they are never coming back, and you might feel overwhelming feelings of loneliness that only add to your already depressed state. Your life is never going to be the same again, and you feel completely alone. This can happen even though you know you have other relatives or friends you still care for. All you can focus on at this stage is the painful loss that you experienced. Depression quickly sets in, and life feels like it makes no sense anymore. Thoughts of suicide might start to creep into your pain when imagining a life without your loved one feels unbearable. Depression is a normal reaction to a devastating loss. As hard as it is to go through this stage, the pain will eventually lift. That is the hope you can hold on to. The pain will eventually ebb away, and you will feel like your old self again. If the depression does become worse instead of better, you must seek out professional help.

- **Stage Seven: Acceptance -** This is the stage that you finally want to reach once you have worked through all your painful emotions. You want to reach a stage in your life where you have accepted the loss. It is a very slow and painful process to get to this stage, but this will also be the stage when you are finally free, and it feels like you can move on with your life. This is the new form that your pain will take, and this new form will be a part of the rest of your life. The loss of a loved one is something you will never truly heal from, but acceptance is when life does go on, and you learn to live with the loss. Acceptance does not mean you are abandoning your loved one, not at all. It simply means that you have accepted their death as a part of your life. Acceptance is a stage where you finally come to the realization that you are going to begin a new life without them in it, a new life that will celebrate the loved one you lost but will never forget. There will be times when you will revert to previous stages of grief for a moment or two, but these painful reminders that pull you back to the despair you felt are a normal part of life. Take comfort in the fact that you will be strong enough by this stage to deal with those moments when they happen.

Grief is mainly affected by four factors:

- **The Relationship That You Had with Them -** The closer you are to the person, the more deeply you will feel that loss. Other factors include how long you had known them and their involvement in your life. Grief is the most painful when it involves a family member because they have been such a fixture in your life that you cannot imagine a life without them. The more meaningful the relationship, the greater the grief.

- **The Way That You Cope -** Some people deal with painful emotions a lot better than others do. Some people may require assistance with coping, while others can manage on their own. It really depends on you and your emotional resilience.

- **Your Personality -** The way you handle your grief can be affected by your personality. It depends on whether you are an introvert or extrovert, whether you are someone who is high strung or easy-going, or whether you are the kind of person that embraces their problems or runs from them. Extroverts might be slightly better at coping than introverts since the extrovert seeks comfort and energy from being around other people. An introvert is less likely to seek out company, even when they are grieving because they have been used to doing most things alone.

- **The Life Experiences You Have Had -** The more life experiences you have related to grief, the better prepared you will be to go through it the next time that it happens. The loss we experience from our past makes it easier to cope with loss in the present.

Knowing the stages of grief can be helpful because it gives you a sense that you are not alone. Others have gone through this same process, and they have survived. This means that you will survive, too, even if it doesn't feel like it right now. Understanding the stages of grief will help should you ever find yourself in a situation where you need to comfort another and help them work through their grief. Every step of the grieving process has meaning to it, and when you are going through these stages, your goal is to work through each of these stages and properly process everything that the stage comes with before you finally move on to acceptance. This is the only way you will be able to move on with your life effectively.

This Is Not Your Fault

As you work through this process, it is important not to turn against yourself. Don't turn the pain of this loss against yourself by ruminating in feelings of guilt and regret. You must remind yourself that none of this is your fault in any way. You know that you did everything you could to save or help your loved one in the best way you knew how, and that is all you can ask for. The last thing that you need during this already difficult process is to turn against yourself. You don't need to beat yourself up over something that cannot be changed.

Be self-compassionate and be kind to yourself. Lean on the people who are closest to you for support. You still have friends, family, and other loved ones whom you care about. They care about you too, and they are going to support you in any way that they can to make this process easier. The single most important thing that you need when a loved one has died is the love and support of other people in your life. It may not replace the love of the person who has died, but it is still the love that you need to hold you up and give you strength in your grief. You are shattered and trying to make sense of something you *cannot make sense of*. One of the complexities of grief is how this pain connects you to the person who died, and it can feel like you are abandoning them when the pain doesn't hurt as much anymore. You don't have to feel guilty about laughing or finding happiness again. You are allowed to feel *both* emotions. You can allow yourself to feel that pain, but at the same time, you can give yourself permission to feel normal once again. It is alright to seek comfort and happiness in your life once more.

Summary

Grief is a process, not a task. Research does show that it is not the circumstances of the death that will predict a negative or positive outcome for any individual. It is the support that they get during this challenging period after death has happened. This is the key component to successfully rebuilding your life after loss. This support could come in many different forms. It could come from a peer support group that you join to talk about your feelings. It could be from talking to friends and family members. Grief is isolating and lonely, and you must reach out and connect with the people you can trust to help you get through it. Grief at the death of a loved one is an all-consuming emotion, and it is essential to look after yourself while you begin to work through the pain. You will always miss and love the people you lost, but the intensity and the overwhelming feeling of the pain will gradually change as the days and years go by. Give yourself as much time as you need to work through this process.

It will help if you remember that grief is a natural and organic process you are not in charge of. You need to let time heal the open wound you feel, even though it sounds like advice that is completely unhelpful when you're feeling such sadness. The only thing you can do is find a way to navigate that process until your pain begins to lessen with each passing day.

Chapter 2: How Is Grief Expressed?

The loss of a loved one can be difficult to talk about, even years after their passing. C.S. Lewis, a best-selling author, once wrote a very powerful opening line in his book entitled *A Grief Observed. "No one ever told me that grief felt a lot like fear."* This is a compelling statement. Grief can feel like fear, but *a fear of what?* Well, when grief and loss hit you, you're afraid of losing yourself, even though you might not be thinking about it at that time. You're fearful of being alone and never being able to fill that hole that they left in your life. If you lose a spouse or partner, you may fear growing old alone. You're afraid that this very intense pain that you feel is never going to stop. You're afraid that you are never going to find happiness again. You're afraid that you are going to forget them, the way they smelled, the way they moved, the sound of their voice, and all the little nuances that you loved about them. You're afraid that others might forget your loved one. Grief can be a very interesting, very powerful, and very complicated emotion. It can make you feel isolated, terrified, depressed, alone, damaged, and scared of everything.

The Effects of Grief

Grief is an emotion and a process that is expressed physically, emotionally, socially, and spiritually. You're going to go through a lot, especially if the loss was a sudden one. Most of us who have not had to deal with grief yet cannot even begin to fathom what it must feel like to have the person you love here one minute and then gone the next with no warning. When we are grieving, we are suffering. Sometimes it feels impossible to have to deal with all these overwhelming thoughts and emotions that have rushed at you like a tidal wave because of the traumatic event you went through. When we are grieving, we don't feel like ourselves at all. We feel disconnected, out of sorts, almost as if we were floating out of our bodies sometimes. Emotionally, physically, and psychologically, your mind and body are going to go through a lot.

Let's take a more in-depth look at how the grieving process can affect you in the following ways:

The Physical Effects of Grief

The pain in your chest will be the most obvious physical evidence that your heart is in pain from the loss. You're quite literally feeling that ache in your chest because the pain is intense enough to cause a physical reaction in your body. Physical effects of grief often include crying, tightness in the chest, headaches, diminished appetite, problems sleeping, weakness, fatigue, aches, pain, and other stress-related experiences. On a physical level, every fiber, muscle, and tissue in your body is absorbing this loss. You're full of aches and pains in your body because you've been impacted so deeply by the loss that you experienced. Sometimes, you might even come down with flu-like symptoms because of the lack of sleep and poor nourishment during this time.

When you are going through the grieving process and not processing your emotions properly, it can lead to physical illness. This is why you must work through the grieving process until you reach the final stage of acceptance. It feels like you have been fragmented like a jigsaw puzzle, and your body doesn't feel like your own. When you block these emotions because you don't want to deal with the pain anymore, that pain will not go away on its own.

When you're hurting but not processing your emotions properly, it can lead to a lot of heart-related issues, high blood pressure from the immense stress that you feel, heart attacks, high cholesterol, respiratory issues, and a lot more. We carry our grief where we carry our stress in life, which explains why you will be prone to frequent headaches during the different stages of your grieving process.

The Social Effects of Grief

When you're going through a difficult period in your life, it can feel like there is nobody out there who will understand you. You may believe that no one can comprehend the sadness and pain that you feel. You don't feel like yourself, and the last thing you want to do is socialize or connect with others while working through your grief. The social effects of grief may include feeling detached from others, isolating, limiting your contact with others, or behaving in ways that are not normal for you. All of this is completely normal because what has happened will turn your world upside down. You will not feel like yourself for several weeks, and sometimes getting a little space, and some time alone might be something you need as you work through this process. Again, this is not going to be the same for everyone. Some people might feel the need to reach out to others more than ever as they make the difficult transition and rebuild their lives.

The Spiritual Effects of Grief

The spiritual effects of grief can be complicated. It could include questioning the reason for your loss, the meaning of life and death, questioning why you had to endure the pain of this loss. This time can also result in anger at God. You question why your loss has to feel incredibly painful, and if your loved one was sick and suffering, you might question why you still feel so angry at God for taking them away from you. If they are finally free from the suffering of this world, shouldn't you be happy for them? You know they are in a better place, and then you begin to feel guilty because you still wish they were here with you. It feels like the stream of love that has been running through your whole life has been dried up.

The Emotional Effects of Grief

Emotional effects of grief include feelings of sadness and deep sorrow accompanied by feelings of worry, anxiousness, frustration, regret, anger, or guilt are also typical. During this process, it can feel as though you are experiencing every single emotion imaginable all at once. It will hit you hard, and it could feel like you have been knocked off your feet. You're going to struggle to stand up again because you feel crippled by these emotions. It will feel as if the crying is never going to stop, and again, this is a completely normal part of the process. Grief and loss are supposed to be very painful, at times, even excruciatingly painful emotions.

The grieving process will be full of these tumultuous emotions because it is not about dealing with loss alone. It is also about coping with *change*. Dealing with the kind of change brought about by loss will take *a lot of time*. The loss of a loved one is a life-changing event, and with every loved one you lose, the cycle is going to start all over again. As difficult as it is, this is a part of life. You should never try to stuff your sorrow away in a place where you don't have to deal with it because this is something that you cannot run away from. Grief is going to be a part of your life at some point or another; therefore, it is crucial to learn how to cope with it. Otherwise, it is always going to feel like a process that is too much to bear.

Dealing with Your Emotions

There is no right or wrong way to deal with the loss of a loved one. When you are broke, feeling broken is the *correct response*. When you are in pain, you *should* be in pain. Being aware of the emotions that may accompany grief is beneficial. If we do not deal with these emotions and they are left unchecked, they can cascade out of control.

Don't be afraid of your pain. You need to let it all in and let the pain run its course. Fighting it, denying it, resenting it, and running away from it is not going to stop the pain from manifesting itself in other aspects of your life. If there is one thing you can expect; it is this: *The grieving process is going to be rough.* When you are grieving, it can feel difficult to hold on to who you are. A lot of your energy is focused on the loss of your loved one, and it's easy to get sucked into the mind space where you can't remember who you are anymore.

To effectively deal with your emotions, you will need to first acknowledge that your pain exists. Taking a moment to focus on ourselves and our thoughts through mindful meditation is a great way to connect our minds and bodies and be more aware of our thoughts and emotions. Often, the feeling of losing control over our thoughts can be just as stressful as the situations we are facing. Regaining control and feeling like you are in control of how your mind and your body responds and reacts to the things you face will help gradually minimize the pain you feel as you work through the stages of grief. When you're experiencing grief, it is easy to forget the things you used to do as part of your routine, and that is how consuming your heartache can be. This is when we fail to eat, sleep, take a shower; perhaps even climbing out of bed feels like an impossible task. When you neglect your physical health, your mental health will be just as affected, and it is already taking a pretty bad hit right now.

As difficult as this time is for you, you need to let the pain in. You need to process your emotions, which is the only way you can take care of yourself. Ignore what society is telling you about suppressing your emotions because that advice is *wrong*. If you choose to follow that advice, instead of learning how to deal with emotions in a healthy way, you're learning instead to suppress them or not talk about them at all. Phrases like “you’ll be fine,” “get over it,” “put on a brave face” are all too common, and they lead to one outcome. The inability to properly manage your emotions, let alone master them. We’ve become so conditioned to think of being emotional as a sign of weakness. That it is unacceptable to show emotion in public and talking about it publicly makes some people uncomfortable. *Forget that advice.* You’ve just lost someone you love, and you’re allowed to feel anything that you want to feel. Scream, shout, let it all out, but the one thing you shouldn’t do is keep it all bottled up inside.

Life isn’t perfect, and there will always be ups and downs, no matter if you are rich or poor. It is when we struggle through the challenges and some of the toughest parts of life, like experiencing grief and loss, that we learn and grow. This is how we become a better and stronger version of ourselves.

Rumi once said this: "*The wound is where the light enters you.*" What a wonderful and profound quote. Essentially, what this quote tells us is that out of darkness comes the light. Imagine yourself as a garden, currently filled with damp and dark soil. It is out of this unpleasant looking soil that beautiful flowers start to blossom and grow. Your grief is like the soil; it is a dark and very painful moment in your life. However, out of this darkness will blossom a beautiful, stronger version of yourself — a person who finds strength during their darkest moments.

When you're dealing with grief and loss, you're emotionally charged. You're dealing with sadness, misery, anger, stress, pain, frustration, and a whole host of other emotions. You experience a wide range of emotions in a short period of time, and it can be very overwhelming if you don't know how to release some of these very painful emotions healthily. Emotions are volatile, constantly changing depending on the situations we find ourselves in and the factors that trigger certain responses. Logic and reason go out the window when intense emotions get involved. The problem is that if you don't learn how to process these emotions now, you run the risk of carrying the emotional baggage with you in the future. You may not think about it right now, but the emotional baggage will always be there, weighing you down. You won't think about it as much, but you will certainly feel the implications of unprocessed emotions. Your future cannot be better if you continue to remain stuck in the past emotionally. Most people don't realize how important it is to work through your emotions as they happen because emotions are not something we consciously think about. Most of it is happening subconsciously at the back of our minds. Even worse, many people will try to suppress their emotions because it doesn't feel good to live with or confront these very painful feelings.

As difficult as they may be, we *need* emotions, painful or otherwise. Our emotions exist to let us know change is happening within our immediate environment or us. Sometimes it alerts us that change could be happening within both. Our emotions supply us with the information that we need about *what* we're experiencing and *how* we should respond to it. Imagine if your emotions shut down and you felt nothing. How would you know what to feel when there was danger present? Or to comfort a loved one when you see them upset? Sure, it is easier to ignore it, sweep it under the rug, or try to suppress it, but it's not healthy. Not even a little bit.

Now, here is something you need to understand about the painful emotions you feel during grief. The loss you experience is going to be part of your past. You can't go back in time to change what has happened, no matter how much you wish you could. You can't go back and rewrite history or change the events that have happened. When an event occurs in our life, we create a story or an interpretation of that event. The story and the interpretation that you create is *where your emotions lie.* This is where the pain, the anger, the guilt, and the frustration and misery that you feel reside. All of those emotions are strongly connected to the story you create in your mind about that specific event. You see, nothing in life has any kind of meaning *except* the meaning that we choose to attach to it. Our brain is always trying to create meaning to make sense of what has happened. In other words, when something is going on in your environment, your brain gets to work trying to interpret what's happening. If that trigger is perceived as a threat, your body goes into the *fight or flight* response mode, and stress hormones like adrenaline and cortisol get pumped into your system. What follows are emotions like anxiety, fear, or in some cases, anger. This will then lead you to choose between two options.

Either you stand your ground and face your fear, or you run.

This means that we have a choice. Even when we're dealing with some of the most painful emotions that we have ever dealt with in our lives, we can *choose* the stories that you create in your life. When you choose to heal from your emotional wounds completely, you create hopeful possibilities for the future. You create hope that everything will be alright again despite the absence of your loved one.

Practical Exercises to Release These Painful Emotions

How do you process and release these painful emotions? With the practical exercises below:

Surrender and Let Go - Letting go sounds like something that is easier said than done, but it can be deceptively effective at helping you work through your painful emotions. The *Letting Go*

Technique was created by David R. Hawkins, author of several books. One of those books was entitled *Letting Go, the Pathway to Surrender.* All you have to do with this exercise is to allow the emotion to come up and let it sit there for a while. You don't have to try and shift it, suppress it, or judge it. All you have to do is let the emotion rise to the surface and let it be. After several moments, let the emotion go.

Surrender and release that emotion. Imagine the emotion was like one of those paper boats you used to fold as a kid. Take that emotion in your hands, look at it for a little while, let it be, and then imagine you're placing that boat in a stream of water and watch it float away. That is how you surrender and release your emotions. Let it float away, just like your little boat on in the stream.

When an emotion comes up, take notice of it, and then let it be. Whenever you notice the emotion, make a note of it and ponder the level of intensity you experience that emotion today. For example, if the emotion of your choice for today is misery, keep tabs on it for the whole day. How often did it happen? Was the feeling strong and intense? The more detailed you are, the more attention it will require from you to properly focus on describing your emotions as accurately as possible.

Emotions will come and go, and things are always changing. The only way an unpleasant or difficult emotion can linger and continue to cause you distress is if you allow it to. It is easy to forget that this feeling will pass, especially when you're enduring emotional turmoil, but this is when you need mindfulness the most. To remind you that all you must do is weather the storm, and it will be over eventually.

Imagine your body was a house, and the unpleasant emotions you feel during this time of grief are the people who are knocking at your door. People you don't want to deal with right now, but the more you try to ignore them, the more persistent they become. Instead of trying your best to ignore them, the learning to let go approach asks that you open the door, invite them in, make them a cup of tea, sit with them for a little while, and then lovingly send them on their way, waving goodbye to those emotions as you do.

The Progressive Muscle Relaxation Exercise - This relaxation technique requires you to focus on slowly tensing each group of muscles. Through this technique, it helps you be more focused on the difference between relaxation and muscle tensions.

You begin by tensing and relaxing the muscles in your toes and then systematically work your way up to the neck and finally to the head. You can also start from your head to the toes, tensing your muscles for five seconds, and then relax for thirty seconds. Through this way, you can become more aware of physical sensations.

Focus on taking deep breaths in and out. Each time you exhale, focus on releasing one muscle area of your body. For example, breathe in deeply, and on the exhale, loosen the muscle in your shoulder area as the air flows out of your body. Take another deep breath in, and on the exhale, relax your arms right down to your fingers. Repeat the process and go through all the areas of your body where you feel tense, progressively relaxing your muscles along the way.

This is also known as the body scan meditation because you could even perform this exercise while you're meditating. This meditation focuses on scanning your own body to release the areas of tension. This meditation aims to notice tension in the body and allows stress to be released.

During this meditation session, you usually begin at one end of the body and work your way throughout. You can start either with your feet and work your way up, or your head and work your way down. With this meditation, you tense and relax each muscle in your body mindfully, and you are also encouraged to visualize peaceful situations.

Progressive muscle relaxation can help you promote generalized feelings of relaxation and calmness, which can help toward the end of your grieving process. You will learn how to slowly and steadily relax your body and also help you sleep better.

Holotropic Breathwork - Holotropic breathing is meant to give you the space you need to let your emotions rise to the surface. Your emotions need to come up in order for them to be released out of your body. This is one way to help your body heal from whatever unprocessed emotion that may be lying underneath the surface.

With this exercise, you are going to sit down in the same position as you would if you are meditating.

You could also choose to lie down and do this if it makes you feel more comfortable. You would then close your eyes and focus on circular breathing. Form the shape of the letter "O" with your lips, and suck in deep breaths while placing both your palms on your stomach area. Keep doing this for as long as you need. You could do it for thirty minutes, sixty minutes, even ninety minutes if you feel like you need it. Do it for as long as you need until you start to feel better emotionally.

While you're performing this holotropic breathing, don't try to suppress any emotions that might come up. If you cry while you do this, it doesn't matter. Let it all out. Let the feelings come and go. You might not always have a big emotional release when you perform this technique, but let it happen if you do.

Learn to Take It Day by Day - Wake up each morning and tell yourself, *"I will take it one day at a time."* Sad times will come and go. Each time you feel overwhelmed with the sadness and depression you feel from your tragic loss. Remind yourself that this storm will pass. There's no magic cure, no formula that is going to take your depression away overnight. The best recovery technique you can start with is to take things one day at a time. Don't try to do too much too soon. Give yourself a break and remember that some things take time. Take it one day at a time, and remember, if you don't succeed today, there is always tomorrow. This darkness will not last forever, not when you keep fighting each day to see the light again.

Practise Gratitude - It's not going to be easy, but if you give your mind something else to focus on other than the immense pain that you feel, this is how you get better day by day. Wake up each morning and find one thing to be grateful for. Use this as your anchor to lead you through the rest of the day. Each time you feel your thoughts starting to get the best of you, return to your reason to be grateful today and concentrate on that until you feel better.

Repeat your reason throughout the day as a reminder that there is at least *one thing* in your life you are still grateful for, even in your darkest moments. One example of something to be grateful for is the support of other loved ones and friends who are by your side during this challenging time. Find something, anything for that matter, that gives you a reason to get up every morning and to keep going. Focus on one to start and gradually work your way up as you begin to feel better.

Emotive Self Vocalization (ESV) - Most people would tell you that you must be crazy if you talk to yourself. But did you realize that you are talking to yourself anyway? You have internal monologue sessions throughout the day from the moment you wake up in the morning. We don't notice it because the voice in our head can be hazy unless it happens to be criticizing us. Then it becomes the inner critic that we don't need in our lives.

The inner monologue you have with yourself daily is always running in the background, filled with repetitive thoughts, judgment, and self-criticism most of the time. Our internal monologue is responsible for affecting our habits, emotions, behaviors, and how we feel during the day. If you have an episode where your emotions seem to be swinging from one extreme to the next, that's probably because of the inner monologue that was happening. You just weren't paying attention to it at that time.

With ESV, you want to vocalize the thoughts that you feel. For example, if you were feeling particularly sad today, ask yourself out loud, *"How am I feeling right now? What is the emotion that I feel? How am I doing? What do I feel about this?"* Answer the questions as though someone else was asking you. Vocalizing your thoughts and emotions will give you unexpected clarity because your thoughts will not be all jumbled and squished together inside your mind. This gives you room to breathe and to finally release some of the thoughts you've had since the passing of your loved one.

Summary

Working through your emotions is something that only you can take responsibility for. Your loved ones and friends can be there to support you, but ultimately, there is only so much they can do to help you. You still need to find a way to help yourself out of your grieving process, and that begins by taking responsibility for and releasing your emotions. If you bottle up all those emotions, then grief is only going to continue manifesting itself in the physical, emotional, and social aspects of your life unless you do something about it. You don't have to rush the process, but you need to accept that this process is something you cannot run away from, no matter how badly you want to.

Chapter 3: The Healing and Coping Process

"The reality is that you will grieve forever. You will not 'get over' the loss of a loved one; you will learn to live with it. You will heal and you will rebuild yourself around the loss you have suffered. You will be whole again but you will never be the same. Nor should you be the same nor would you want to."

—Elisabeth Kubler-Ross

Be patient because there is no quick fix. Losing the one you love is a difficult process. It certainly feels like you've lost them, but they are never *truly* lost because they remain a permanent part of your life. Nothing you can do in your life will ever prepare you for that inevitable day when you have to say goodbye. Everything that you have ever learned before this about how to deal with having your heart broken will not help you when it comes to grief. That is because grief is a different kind of pain. Despite being an inevitable process of life, we were never taught how to grieve properly.

The day you lose the one you love will change your life forever. How do you heal from something like that? The first time we deal with grief is when we realize just how naive about it we were. We thought we could anticipate what the process would be like, but nothing could even come close to preparing you for it. Feeling strong feels like the impossible thing to do at this point, and that is alright. The healing and coping process is going to come at a much later stage. For now, all you need to know are the steps that will prepare you when it's time for you to heal. The steps that will tell you the best way to recover from such a painful event.

You Need to Take Care of Yourself

During the grieving process, you need to take care of yourself. Take the time to be attentive to your mental, physical, and emotional needs. The healing process and taking care of yourself doesn't have to feel forced, and it doesn't necessarily have to be all about meditation or yoga either. Self-care during the grieving process is all about honoring the grief that you are feeling right now. It is about trying to work that self-care strategy into the grieving process and allow it to happen simultaneously.

Here are some examples of what you could do:

- **Explore Nature -** Studies have shown that being outside in nature can do wonders when it comes to minimizing the stress and the pressure that you feel. You don't have to walk if you don't feel like it. If the weather permits, sit outside in the warm sunshine and let the fresh air surround you. Close your eyes and listen to the sounds of nature for a minute, allow your mind to be free and still, and don't think about anything else except what you can hear. If you have a bike, go for a bike ride outside. You're moving faster and going further, and it could be one way to take your mind off things for a little while as you pay attention to the road.

- **Pick Up the Phone and Call A Friend** - The number one way to look after your mental health is to turn to the comfort of a friend. If you don't feel ready for any physical contact just yet, pick up the phone and let the voice of someone you love and care about fill your ears and your soul. You could even text them if that is all that you feel ready for. The grieving process is entirely up to you and what you think works best. Ask them if you could vent your feelings for a little bit, or if you don't feel like talking, let them do all the talking by asking them about their day. Whenever your mind feels like it can't take anymore, talk to someone about it. The clutter you feel mentally results from all the thoughts and emotions you have squished up there together with no place to go. This is perfectly normal because you probably spent the first few days or weeks after your loved one has passed grieving about them alone. Your emotions are up and down and all over the place, and whenever the burden feels like it is too much to carry on your own, reach out and talk to someone about it. Let these emotions go by getting things off your chest. Talk about it because it feels better knowing you're not alone and you've got people who care about you. Talking about it with someone you trust could even bring an added benefit with it. You get to brainstorm solutions, and you'll end up feeling much better by the end of that heart-to-heart. Companionship is key, and you should seek support from safe people who do not judge you or tell you how to grieve.

- **Seek A Creative Outlet -** One of the best creative outlets you could turn to is music. Music is healing for many people. Turn on any kind of music that you feel like listening to. Some people find classical music relaxing and helpful. Maybe you feel like listening to some angry music to let go of some of that anger and frustration that you feel.

- **Write In A Journal -** Writing and journaling are tried and true tactics that many have found beneficial over the years. Some people find comfort in journaling to their loved one who has passed, pouring out their heart and soul and everything they wish they could say to them. Ultimately, the purpose of this journal is to help you get your emotions and your thoughts out there instead of having them bottled up inside your head. If you don't feel comfortable expressing your grief to anyone else, then a journal is an excellent option for you. Get your thoughts out of your head and put them on a piece of paper or a notebook. Journaling is a great way to help keep you on the right track towards recovery. Journaling promotes a state of mindfulness because when you're writing down everything you are feeling, you are acknowledging your thoughts and paying attention to them. Instead of letting your mind wander and your thoughts get out of control, writing them down in a response journal will force you to bring them into focus, especially when you ask yourself questions in the journal and then attempt to answer them. Reading everything you have read later on from an objective perspective is one way to encourage kindness to yourself. No doubt you would have been too hard on yourself during this challenging time, and you probably didn't realize it until you reflected on what you wrote during the peak points of your grief. A journal can be extremely effective because you feel lighter after "unburdening" yourself, the same way that you feel better after talking to a friend. Expressing your emotions, especially the things you may not be comfortable revealing to others just yet, has been known to reduce and lower anxiety and stress levels. Even if the only one seeing the journal is you, you just feel better about letting it all out.

- **Read or Watch Something Funny -** There is nothing wrong with finding a reason to laugh again. Allow yourself to set grieving aside for a while; don't obsess on the loss for any longer than necessary. It is alright to take a break, work, laugh, and have fun when you can. When you are grieving, you are in the depths of some of the darkest emotions in your life. If this is your first experience with loss, then it is probably some of *the* gloomiest days you have ever had to deal with up to this point. Whenever you need to get your mind off things, put your favorite TV show or funny movie on as a distraction. Allow yourself to get lost in what you're watching and laugh again. Nothing is simpler or more effective and instantaneously making you feel better and unburdening yourself from some of those stressful emotions. Laugh, and remember that it is alright to laugh hard. Be around people who make you love.

Watch your favorite comedies or movies, watch comedy specials, anything that is going to get you laughing in a genuine, carefree manner.

- **Try and Sigh** - Take a deep breath and just let out the biggest sigh you can. Do that as many times as you need. Breathing is one of the many underrated exercises that can be extremely beneficial in helping to release some of those pent up emotions. That big, giant sigh is going to bring some sense of relief. As you sigh, imagine that every tense and stressful emotion that you feel now is exhaling out of your body. You'd be surprised at how much better you will feel after doing this a couple of times.

Create a Ritual to Honor Those Who Have Passed

Guilt is one of the most powerful emotions that many people struggle with when it comes to grief recovery. They believe that by healing and not crying as much over their loved ones anymore, they have somehow "abandoned" them or "forgotten" about them. To help you overcome this stage, you can create rituals that honor the people you've lost. Carry on the little traditions that you used to enjoy doing together. It doesn't have to stop just because they are no longer around. If they loved watching movies together with you every Saturday night, keep that little ritual going, and you could invite a friend or family member over if it feels too much to be alone right now.

Simplify Your Life

There will be a lot going on inside you during the grieving process, and the last thing you need is to have physical clutter in your external environment. When you're already struggling to get through the day without breaking down in tears, it is essential to do what you can to make your life as simple as possible.

In other words, you need to declutter your life, remove anything that is unnecessary, and avoid making tough decisions for the time being. This is not something you have to do alone if it feels overwhelming. Decluttering is a process that can be done by enlisting the help of a friend. When someone we love dies, some people might go through a process known as “grief hoarding.” Grief hoarding happens when we try to cling on to the items that used to belong to the one we lost, and hoarding takes place when we can’t figure out what to discard.

Relax, you don’t have to do everything in a single day. Deciding what to keep and what to get rid of is challenging, and this is not something you need to tackle right away if you’re not up for it yet. But at some point, part of the healing process is going to involve some decluttering. By simplifying our lives, we enable ourselves to cut ties with additional material attachments and cultivate a calmer and peaceful mind.

Simplify your life and the things that you do. Eliminating the physical clutter from your life is an excellent place to start, but simplifying the things that you do extends to your social life, work schedule, and all the other daily tasks that you usually find yourself occupied with. Simplify the clutter in your schedule by listing your commitments down and then picking a few of the most important ones to get done in a day. Avoid over-cluttering and scheduling commitments back to back. Allow some breathing space and time for yourself in between to process your emotions.

This should be your focus during the first initial weeks of losing your loved one. Trying to keep busy to avoid the pain of having to confront these emotions will never be a healthy approach. In your attempt to be busy, you might end up complicating your life and creating even more stress to deal with. The purpose of this decluttering exercise is to give you that sense of equilibrium and give yourself time to rebuild strength.

Finding Acceptance

Grief can be even harder when you try to suppress and push down all those emotions you don't want to feel. Your heart is breaking at the devastating loss, and it will feel as though you are never going to smile again. You don't have to do it right away; you can take your time working toward the acceptance stage. Several times along the way, as you work through the stages of grief, you might experience some sense of disbelief. You cannot believe that this happened, especially if the death of your loved one was sudden and shocking.

Acceptance is the completion of the journey you had with your loved one. You've walked with them for a period in your life, and now it is time to continue walking down the path of life without them. Maybe it is something you don't feel ready for or something that you don't want to do, but either way, it is your new reality.

If you keep fighting it, the recovery process is only going to be that much harder. Cry about it, scream about it, shout, and let it all out, but you need to accept it. It will feel like the journey you took with your loved one was cut short, but remember that your loved one will never truly leave your side. They will always hold a very special place in your heart. You walked with them for a while, and now it is time to close that chapter and go forward to the next stage. Once you have reached acceptance, the knife that felt like it was stabbed into your chest when you lost the one you love is going to slowly start backing away.

Summary

Grief is a normal and natural reaction to a loss of any kind. Grief happens in your heart, but the broken pieces of your heart will mend again one day. Have faith that grieving leads to healing and personal growth. Recognize and honor the healing process for what it is, and don't fight the emotions you will feel during this time. If you ever find yourself in a state where you feel "stuck," remember that it is alright to seek help. Everyone could use a helping hand once in a while, and this could be the time when you need to reach out to someone to help you through the process. The bottom line is, you need to do whatever it takes not to give up. You will feel like your old self again, and it is only a matter of time. For now, what you need to do is be patient and have faith, follow the steps and go through this stage by stage, and eventually, you will reach that final stage of acceptance.

CHAPTER 4: TAKING CARE OF YOURSELF

"Accept yourself, love yourself, and keep moving forward. If you want to fly, you have to give up what weighs you down." - Roy T. Bennett

The grieving process can be exhausting, surreal, and confusing. It can leave you feeling completely and utterly lost. You may *think* you understand grief, but when you go through it, you realize perhaps you didn't understand it as well as you hoped you did. For one thing, you probably had no idea that the pain of grief could be so physical that it feels like it could kill you. You had no idea that all the pain you would feel could be more overwhelming than sadness. There was no way you could anticipate that experiencing the loss of a loved one could make you feel like a stranger in your own home. You had no idea that it could make you feel cut off from the person that you were or that you could feel disconnected from the people closest to you. We simply had no idea how powerful this feeling of grief could be.

When you're grieving a significant loss, it cannot be stressed enough how you don't have to go through this process alone; it is normal to need help getting you out of the darkness. At a crucial time like this, perhaps you need a little help to remind you that you should not neglect yourself. In fact, this is the time you should be taking care of yourself more than ever.

Be Patient With Yourself

Don't become overburdened in your grief. Grief is a process that is very disorientating and exhausting. You're probably not going to feel like yourself for several weeks, depending on how quickly you get through the stages of your grief and the support you have. Be gentle and kind, and keep your expectations realistic. Don't listen to what others tell you *they think* you should do. You do what feels right for you. There will be moments when you experience frustration because progress to recovery seems slow, or you may be frustrated with the people around you because they are not giving you the help in the way that you want or expect.

Be patient because overcoming grief is going to take time. You need to be patient with yourself, and eventually, you will get there. As for the people around you, be patient with them too because they are learning just as you are about what they can do to help. Even physical wounds take time to heal. Be patient with yourself every step of the way, and trust the process. You will get there eventually, and keeping your expectations realistic during this time is how you take care of your mental health.

Be kind, compassionate, and gentle to yourself. You have been through an experience that has left a deep wound in your heart, and you will need an empathetic, compassionate inner voice to help you work through the process.

You Don't Have to Make Any Major Decisions or Choices

You will be exhausted, and you will not be in the right frame of mind to make any kind of decision. If you don't feel up for it, you don't have to do it. There is absolutely no pressure at all, except the one you may be placing on yourself. This is why it is important to be kind and realistic. The last thing you need is to create even more stress with an already stressful situation.

Give Yourself Some Space and Some Time to Grieve

You don't have to pretend that you are not in a lot of pain. You don't have to pretend that everything is alright because it is *not* alright. It is never going to be alright losing the people that we love. Give yourself as much time and space as you need to grieve properly, and you don't have to do anything that you are not ready for. This is part of the self-care process that we talked about in the earlier chapter. When you're giving yourself this time and space, this is when you should attempt to write in your journal. This is one of the many rituals you can create to help you go through this period.

Give Yourself Permission

It is alright to set aside the grieving process for a while. You can permit yourself to do that without having to feel bad. You need to do things to make yourself happy. Otherwise, those dark and negative emotions can quickly fast-track you on the road to depression. It is alright to work, find some time to relax, start having fun again with your friends and family, and above all else, it is alright to laugh and find joy in the little things in life once more.

Life does go on, and you can be sure that your loved one wouldn't want you to be miserable for the rest of your life either. They would want you to be happy again, and if you ever find yourself feeling awash with guilt, think about that.

You will absolutely need moments where you need to take a break from all the crying for a little while to recharge your batteries. Overcoming the stages of grief is a long and slow road, and you are going to need all the energy you can get.

Seek Support from Safe People

"Safe people" is the key phrase in this step. You need to surround yourself with people who are not going to judge or criticize you. The safe people in your life could be your friends and family or a grief counselor if you feel that you need a little more help than your circle of support can offer you right now.

Find support and seek comfort in people who know how to listen empathetically without trying to say what they *think* will help snap you out of it. Seek comfort in the people with the ability to listen with compassion and demonstrate kindness for the plight of others. Empathic listening skills may seem like an easy thing to find amongst friends and family, but nothing could be further from the truth. Mostly, the challenge lies in the fact that most people find it hard not to let preconceived notions or biases cloud their judgments. A lot of people would rather talk about what's interesting or beneficial for them. To be able to listen entirely to the plight of another with nothing in it for you, that is a selfless act, and it is often even more difficult to master than your basic listening skills. It requires you to literally walk a mile in the person's shoes by experiencing every emotion that they are. You get to feel their happiness, sadness, anguish, joy, misery, the challenges that they face, almost as though you were the one going through their journey too.

You will often find that the ones who have suffered a similar loss will be the people you find easiest to talk to. It is alright to seek out a counselor or professional help if you feel that your immediate circle is not equipped with the kind of support you need at this time.

Find Things to Be Grateful For

One thing you will need to accept is that your life is going to feel crazy for a little while. Snapping out of it is not an option, pretty much the same way that wishing the pain would go away will not change anything. When it comes to the grief process, there are no shortcuts through the pain. You have to gradually work through the process, and it is going to be incredibly helpful if you can find little things to be grateful for every day.

For example, you can feel grateful every day for the family and friends you still have around you. There's nothing that reminds you of how much you have to be thankful for, like connecting with the people you love. These are the ones who make you feel safe, secure, and understood. Connecting with your loved ones is a natural stress reliever for both the mind and body. They may not be able to fix your stress entirely, but being in their company, talking about something else other than your worries, maybe even laughing and having a good time, can wash away all the unpleasant thoughts you were struggling to shake.

Feeling grateful for the little things you have every day is how you restore your faith that grief will eventually lead to healing. Despite the suffering, there is still a lot left in your life to be thankful for. Be grateful you woke up this morning healthy. Be grateful you got to work safely. Be grateful you had the means to buy food and drink when you were hungry. Be grateful for another productive day at work. Spend every waking moment being grateful for all the little things in your life, especially the things we tend to overlook. Reminding yourself to be grateful is an exercise that will help restore your faith and shake the negative emotions. It slows you down long enough to stop and appreciate what you were reminding yourself to be grateful for.

Handle Your Negative Emotions

Negative emotions can make you feel hopeless. As long as these negative emotions and thoughts continue to linger in your mind, hope will always be something elusive and difficult to find. During your grief, it can be easy to quickly develop a negative mindset because a lot of the subconscious thoughts we have happens on autopilot. We're not thinking about it as much as we should be. We ignore how destructive and damaging these thoughts can be until we wake up one morning and wonder how we became so negative.

Believing that your negative thoughts are true without *challenging* them is how you gradually develop a negative mindset that can be hard to shift. You will feel your thoughts spiraling toward the negative even more when you're working through the grieving process.

Part of taking care of yourself during this time will be to surround yourself with as much positive material as you possibly can. For example, you could use positive affirmations and read or listen to inspirational and uplifting content. Positive affirmations were underestimated for a long time until research suggested that they are powerful tools that could significantly decrease stress and help you feel positive about yourself. It is one of the many techniques used by successful people to shift their thinking away from negativity to remain focused on their goals. Aim for content that is going to help put a smile on your face. Aim for positive affirmations that remind you of what you're capable of can be empowering.

For more information about handling negative emotions and negative thinking, you should check out my book: How to Stop Being Negative, Angry, and Mean: Master Your Mind and Take Control of Your Life.

Use Visualization

Visualization is a coping method that uses visual imagery to ease sorrow during periods of isolation. Visualization is an empowering method that can motivate you to stay on track. It is an excellent "mind strengthening exercise" to direct your subconscious to what you want. This process is about purposefully creating a crystal clear mental image in your mind of *what you want* to see manifest into your reality.

Visualize yourself feeling happy again in the

future, even without the physical presence of your loved one. Imagine yourself going through your days stronger and happier. Visualize the moments that you used to share with your loved one and smile when you do as you immerse yourself in the memory of the life you once shared.

Recognize the relationship between the mind and body

Your physical health matters just as much as mental health does. The mind and body are connected as a unit, and what affects one will undoubtedly affect the other. As soon as you are up for it, make time to include exercise into your recovery routine. It doesn't have to be anything too vigorous to start with. Something as simple as going for a walk is enough to ease you into the process.

Exercises help not only to elevate your mood, but as your body gets fitter and healthier, your energy levels will increase, and you'll find you're able to accomplish so much more in a day. Exercising also helps boost your endorphin levels, which allows you to feel good and feel happy. Exercising is an outlet for you to let out any frustration or stress you may have so that it isn't bottled up inside you.

Those who work out regularly will be able to attest to how much better they feel after they've done a workout. As you work through the stages of your grief, rely on exercise as an excellent tool that can help teach you how to manage your stress and release and let go of any current stress you may be carrying around with you.

Understanding the interactions of others

The people in your life who are reaching out to you are not trying to hurt you. They feel just as lost as you do, and they sometimes don't know what the right thing to say may be. That is because there *will* never be a "right thing" to say when you're dealing with the loss of a loved one. As much as your family and friends love you, they are also afraid of saying the wrong thing at this time that might trigger certain emotions within you. They're *afraid* of your feelings since not everyone is going to be comfortable with the idea of speaking about death. Death is not an easy subject to discuss in any context, and when you are dealing with someone who is vulnerable and in a lot of pain at the moment, death can be an even more complicated subject to deal with.

It's not that your loved ones don't want to help you, because they do. If they could take away your pain, you can be sure that they would. At times, the things they say might seem insensitive, but they have good intentions behind them, even if it doesn't come out that way.

Summary

When you feel lost, ask yourself, *"What do I need to do to take care of myself right now?"*. Every step in this chapter is meant to serve as a guide to help you get started on the self-care process. No matter what it is that you decide you need to help you feel better, it is essential to follow through. Do it because your self-care and your recovery will depend on it.

A Short Message from the Author

Hey, are you enjoying the book? I'd love to hear your thoughts!

Many readers do not know how hard reviews are to come by and how much they help an author.

I would be incredibly thankful if you could take just 60 seconds to write a brief review, even if it's just a few sentences!

Chapter 5: The Power of Gratitude

"Enjoy the little things, for one day you may look back and realize they were the big things." - Robert Brault

Gratitude and giving thanks are among the most powerful things you can practice. If you can hold on to gratitude even in your darkest and lowest moments in life, it can get you through anything. It is no secret that gratitude is the answer to lasting happiness, and the happiest people you will ever meet will always be the ones who walk about with gratitude oozing out of every pore. You will know who they are because they will always be talking about the power of gratitude.

Gratitude is the feeling of being blessed. It is the ability to appreciate the things you already have instead of focusing on what you lack. That gratitude drives those who are grateful every day, and that is how they continue to attract even more good things into their life. If you think about all the things you have to be grateful for, most of the time it is going to be for the things that money can't buy. Gratitude for the loving family that you have been blessed with, for example. Gratitude for the friends and the people in your life that you love and care deeply about. Appreciation for your good health and wellbeing, and gratitude for the mental health that keeps you strong when you're faced with monumental challenges. Gratitude for the courage not to give up even though you may have wanted to several times along the way. You're still here, still standing, and still strong, and this is something to be grateful for every day. Gratitude for the inner strength you didn't know you had as you overcame the pain you feel from grief and loss.

Those are the kind of blessings that encompass what gratitude is all about. It is not about money all the time. Money doesn't last forever because it comes, and it goes. Gratitude is one of the healthiest positive emotions that we can feel as a person. Those who are always grateful every day somehow seem like they are more resilient to stress, and there is a very good reason for it. Not only does gratitude actively remind you of the things you have to be grateful for, but when you actively remind yourself of all the good experiences you have in your life. It helps to magnify positive thoughts, and soon, the positive thoughts will eventually be strong enough to overpower the negative and toxic emotions.

Gratitude During Grief

When you're grieving, it will seem impossible that you will make it through the other side. Somewhere in the back of your mind, you know that you will reach that point one day, but it can feel unbearable during that peak grieving period. Your whole world has been turned upside down, and probably the last thing on your mind is finding the will to be grateful each day. How do you feel grateful when you just lost someone you love? You can't even fathom being thankful when you're in such deep, immense pain. How do you even think about gratitude at a time like this? Could grief and gratitude really be compatible? Or is gratitude something that comes later after you've passed the stage of acceptance?

It's not going to be easy, and that is the truth. This will probably be one of the hardest things you have to do, and it will require conscious effort each day. It will take a lot of determination and willpower to find that one good thing to latch on to each day to feel grateful about. It's going to start with just one thing, and even that is going to feel difficult. Eventually, as you begin to heal and reach the stage of acceptance, it will increase from one thing to two things, then three, four, five, and more.

Think about what your loved one would want for you. Would they want you to dwell in misery, mourning their loss for the rest of your life? Or would they want you to be grateful and happy and go on with your life with a smile? Yes, the pain you feel right now is incredibly powerful, but so is your determination to overcome it. The power of gratitude will be the force that gets you through this storm in a way that nothing else ever will. Your family and friends can try their best to cheer you up, and if you don't have that passion that is created by gratitude, negativity is always going to pull you back into its fold.

Gratitude is something that happens now, and it happens every day. It is not something that happens later, and it is not something that happens when things are going well in your life. By practicing gratitude while you grieve, it can help you cope with those painful emotions. Research shows that those who practice gratitude all the time feel a lot less lonely and isolated than those who didn't practice gratitude at all. They had more compassion for themselves and others. Those who practice gratitude regularly will find it slightly easier to mitigate all the emotions that come with the grieving process.

The ability to express gratitude every day is something that takes work. During the grieving process, it is going to require even *more* work. We have been trained for most of our lives to see problems more than solutions, negatives rather than positives. We focus on what's lacking, what's not good enough, instead of taking the time to appreciate all the good that we have going on. We end up becoming more critical than grateful.

When you're grieving, you need gratitude more than ever. The ability to be grateful is such a powerful force that it can help block out some of those strong negative emotions you will experience during the grieving process. Emotions like resentment and regret are just some of the many emotions that will flood your mind and body during the grieving process, and without gratitude, it's easy to spiral down the rabbit hole. In a way, getting into that space of being grateful each day will give you some reprieve from the many emotions you will have to work through.

Gratitude helps you rewire your brain for positive thinking, and someone who consistently practices positive thinking is someone who can bounce back much faster from any adversity in life. Those who practice gratitude will never have to wonder whether there will be a light at the end of this dark tunnel of loss. That is because they *know for a fact* that the light is waiting for them on the other side. All they have to do is make the trip through this tunnel.

Gratitude Gives You the Power You Seek

Gratitude every day is going to give you a sense of intervention. It will be the secret weapon that will provide you with power in a time that may seem powerless. When you are grieving, you are vulnerable, and it can feel like there will be many things happening to you in that moment that you cannot control. You may not have control, but there is something that you do have. *You have a choice.* Practicing gratitude means you are exercising that power of choice.

It is a good idea to write down your blessings on a list so you can pull it out anytime you need a reminder about how fortunate you are. When life gets in the way with its unending obstacles and unexpected curveballs, it becomes easy to get caught up in the "why always me" mentality and forget that you have more reasons to smile than to frown, despite the challenges that may be in front of you right now. The hard times never last for long, and when you remember all that you should be grateful for and practice gratitude each day, you'll be able to weather any storm without losing your happiness in the process.

Marcus Aurelius shared a pearl of wisdom with us: *"When you wake up each day, remember what a precious gift and privilege it is that you are alive."* This is an incredibly profound thought and one that not many of us remember to be grateful for. Being alive is an incredible thing, and each new day brings with it the opportunity for you to choose to do something better with your life. To make the choices that fuel your focus and bring greater clarity in the quest to accomplish your goals. Aurelius was not the only one to recognize the incredible power behind this thought. When you remember what a gift it is to be alive, be strong, healthy, and in control of your destiny, choosing to focus on the essential things that bring greater happiness and purpose in your life becomes the obvious choice to make.

Practicing gratitude during your grief may seem impossible, but it can be done. The key is you must be intentional; purposely choose things in your life to feel thankful for, and these should be things that bring up genuine feelings of gratitude. For example, feeling grateful that you still have other loved ones in your life to turn to. There is the power to be found in expressing genuine gratitude for everything you have in your life. It lifts your spirits and fills you with happiness, which improves your satisfaction levels. It helps you remember all the little blessings you should be thankful for that can easily be forgotten and taken for granted. Practice an attitude of gratitude every day and look at what a difference it can make in your life. It can do wonders for your healing process.

Perhaps you could dedicate your gratitude practice to your lost loved one over the next several weeks. For gratitude to have those powerful and positive effects on your life, it needs to be something that you do consistently. It is just like exercising, where you have to put in the time to build those muscles. Gratitude is something that will become second nature, but only through consistent repetition. When you're trying to create this habit of becoming more grateful, your daily practice must be rooted in something meaningful. This will be the foundation that will create long-lasting change. When it comes from a place of meaning, there will be less mental resistance because you're genuine about what you do. When you connect the practice with something personal and something that holds deep meaning for you, it gives you something to focus on. By dedicating your gratitude practice to your lost loved one, you're strengthening the connection and re-establishing the relationship you had with them. Just because your loved one is not around anymore, it doesn't mean that you have to lose the connection you had with them.

Gratitude Habit Stacking

If gratitude is something new that you're trying, it helps to associate it with a habit that already exists. This technique is called *habit stacking.* Habit stacking works by first identifying an existing routine and adding a *new habit* on top of that existing habit.

These should be habits you do daily without even being told twice or having to think about it, so these are your existing habits. Habit-stacking requires that you link your *new desired habit* to an existing one. Essentially, what you're trying to do is make an existing habit a trigger for your new habit. You can choose to carry out this new habit either before or after your existing habit, as long as it works for you.

Make gratitude part of your routine because it will

do wonders to get you through this challenging time in your life. It will change the relationship that you have with grief when you find even the simplest of reasons to get out of bed in the morning. It is what your loved one would have wanted for you. Right now, it may seem like you have lost everything, but you *haven't.* There is still so much of life to be lived, and there is still a lot of love in your life.

Summary

Gratitude is a form of self-care, and this is the time when you need to do everything you can to look after yourself. Gratitude is a beautiful gift that you can give yourself regularly at a time when you desperately need it. Gratitude can also be a way of extending the relationship you had with your loved one beyond the physical realm. It helps if you piggyback this new habit you are trying to form onto an existing habit to make it stick.

Chapter 6: Roadblocks to Overcoming Grief

Losing someone near and dear to us causes an avalanche of feelings and emotions. From shock to anger to regret, pain, sadness, grief, and depression, and finally, acceptance. Why did this happen? How could this happen? Why did I not stop this from happening? I shouldn't have said this to him/her last night! All of these thoughts mingled with the various emotions are bound to be felt by a person grieving, and it is hard to dissect each of these elements to try to figure them out.

How the mind thinks and processes information during this terrible time is hard to comprehend, let alone understand. The reality of grief is that it's very complex, and it can come with several roadblocks along the way.

What is a Grief Roadblock?

A grief roadblock refers to a state of complicated and challenging emotions that stand in the way of a healthy grieving process. These roadblocks lead the bereaved into a rollercoaster of emotions and often prevents them from moving forward in life. Understandably, anger, guilt, and regret will sometimes take over the landscape of emotions when a person loses someone. Still, while they are very different emotions, the actions taken to push past them are similar.

Getting ‘stuck’ at some point in the grieving process is common and likely. However, when anger, guilt, and regret consume and manifest themselves in every aspect of a person’s life, that’s when it breeds trouble. These emotions can prevent a person from looking beyond the grief and pain and instead develop destructive patterns.

Let's explore some common roadblocks to overcoming grief:

- **Anger**- Anger is either directed at the medical profession for not ‘doing enough’ to ensure that the deceased was well cared for. It could also be directed to the cause of death. It could even be directed at family and friends for not being supportive. It could be anger at the deceased or anger with God, a disease, or a drug. A grieving person can and will find anything to direct their anger towards until they come to terms with what has happened.

- **Guilt**- Guilt creeps in when the bereaved feel like they were not able to do more. This 'more' can be anything from giving extra care, answering the last call, not getting help in time, not stopping the deceased from doing something that may have led to their death.

- **Regret**- This feeling takes place when the bereaved feel that they 'should have or could have' done something to prevent death from happening. It could also be the last few things they said or didn't say, did or didn't do.

- **Self Pity**- It's natural to withdraw and mend after a devastating loss; however, with self-pity, you excessively dwell on yourself and your sorrows. You see yourself as the victim and the only person suffering. It's essential to understand the differences between self-pity and grief so that healing can take place.

- **Self-destructive behaviors**- Self-destructive behavior is described as actions we do that are sure to cause harm to ourselves. With grief often comes pain, anger, or sadness - all emotions that people will naturally want to avoid. Some people resort to self-destructive behaviors such as taking drugs or alcohol to deal with these undesirable emotions. If we use drugs or alcohol to numb the pain we feel, we do not learn how to cope with sadness and grief. We don't naturally allow ourselves to go through the process of grieving. Furthermore, problems arise when this behavior becomes a habit; it can lead to depression, substance abuse, or other destructive behaviors such as over-eating, under-eating, and more.

- **Isolation**- When we grieve, it can feel compelling to keep people at arm's length so we don't get hurt. But at what cost do we do this? Isolation can make feelings of grief and loneliness even more intense. Isolation can also make it harder to process grief. The sense of isolation usually comes up when we feel like we don't belong. While everyone else is feeling happy, celebrating a birthday, socializing with friends, we can feel extremely isolated because we think nobody else feels the pain we are going through. When this happens, frustration creeps in, and it is usually accompanied by irrational isolation. Studies have shown that prolonged isolation can have many adverse side effects on the human mind.

- **Fear**- Experiencing and healthily processing all emotions is crucial for the grieving process. Fear in this aspect is not merely the fear of dying. Instead, it's the fear of whether the bereaved can go through life without the deceased. This fear can create destructive patterns in our minds. Obsessing over life without the deceased only reinforces the impact of the negative thoughts and emotions. You fear not being able to work properly, not being able to take care of your children, not doing a particular activity that caused the death of the loved one. Sometimes, it is easy to suppress our feelings and not think about them, especially painful and scary memories. But as we all know, stuffing your memories and feelings will only make things worse for you.

- **Unforgiveness**- To forgive someone is the ability to pardon an offense without holding any grudges or resentment. When we experience loss, we tend to get angry at the reason or cause of the deceased's death-it could be someone, something, or an event. We hold that person or thing responsible, and we find something or someone to direct our anger. We resent them, and because of this, it makes it harder for us to let go of what has been. We blame them for death and loss, and we can't seem to forgive them. This resentment builds up and, without intervention, it makes it harder to forgive. Without forgiveness, it becomes a massive roadblock on your journey to recovery.

- **Substance Abuse Relapse** - Sudden grief often triggers addicts to relapse.

These roadblocks cause a vicious cycle in the bereaved's mind and prevent them from moving forward. This cycle needs to be broken because it is unhealthy, and it stops us from living our lives past the deceased.

9 Common Myths and Misconceptions About Grief

1. Grief has an endpoint.

Over time, the pain of grief diminishes and becomes less pronounced; however, for most, it never completely goes away. We learn to adjust and grow with it. While grief has no endpoint, it, however, will feel different and become more manageable. But it will always be there.

2. Everyone grieves the same way.

No, they don't. Everyone experiences grief differently. Grief does not decide the sequence in which bereaved people experience the various stages of grief and loss. It's quite common for people to skip or cycle through these different emotions and feelings and sometimes miss a stage altogether. You might feel sad, but then you might think that you've accepted that the deceased is gone. But somewhere along the road, you might go back to denial or even anger.

3. The pain will be less if you act like it never happened.

Unfortunately, acting like it never happened only means you are bottling up your feelings and not acknowledging that something terrible has happened. You are not letting yourself feel grief, pain, or loss. You're refusing to accept the reality of the situation, and this itself is unhealthy. At some point, when reality hits, it will hit hard, and everything will come crashing down unexpectedly, preventing yourself from coping with the magnitude of the pain and loss that you've kept bottled up all this while. So allow yourself to feel the pain, allow yourself to feel the loss, and allow yourself to grieve.

4. Your grief should last for a specific period.

As mentioned in previous chapters, there is no specific time with grief. Expecting someone to 'get over it' or saying 'it's already been two years' or even 'You should be done grieving by the end of the year' only puts pressure on the bereaved, causing other unhealthy obsessions and destructive behaviors. A person grieving will go through various emotions, and adding a timeline only adds to the stress.

5. Grief support groups will make you more depressed.

Grief support groups help you to cope and enable you to connect with people who have experienced grief from a loved one's death. Grief support groups are helpful once funeral arrangements, legal matters, and other financial issues have been sorted. Once the dust has settled slightly, it helps to join grief support groups to connect and find support. It may not work so well if the bereaved doesn’t feel like talking about the deceased's death, prefers to mourn in silence, or chooses to be left alone for a bit. These support groups come with a professional therapist or group leader to help steer the conversation to promote healthy habits and coping skills so that no one falls into depression.

6. God needed them in Heaven.

Calling a tragic loss the "will of God" can have a devastating impact on the faith of the bereaved. It’s not something they would want to hear. Nobody knows where people go after they die, and to make this assertion implies that you are trying to shove your beliefs on them. Whether you believe it or not, it’s not the right thing to say at all to someone who just recently lost someone. At that point, all the bereaved wants is to have their loved one next to them.

7. If you don't cry, it means you are not sorry for the loss.

As mentioned before, everyone grieves differently. Grief manifests in different ways. Some people look resilient in the face of a crowd and prefer crying alone in their room. Some people make jokes as it reminds them of the deceased or helps them deal with the pain. Some people stay quiet as they are still in shock at what happened.

8. Grief is only felt by family and friends close to the deceased.

Grief is felt by anyone with an emotional attachment to the deceased. It doesn't matter whether you know the person or not. Take, for example, our emotional response to a celebrity's death from Michael Jackson to Princess Diana. Each of us had a varying degree of emotional connection to them, and we all grieved in different ways. No doubt it hits the hardest for close friends and family members, but grief is felt by anyone and everyone who feels connected to the deceased.

9. Moving on with your life means that you are forgetting about the one you lost.

Again, this is a myth that needs to be binned. Grief has no endpoint, and neither is there a specific timeline everyone should follow. Moving on is a healthy outcome of grief. It means that you've overcome the grief roadblocks, you've accepted that your loved one is gone, and you are ready and brave to take the next steps into crafting life without your loved one. They are still etched in your memory and every time you taste, feel, smell or hear something that reminds you of them, instead of crying, you smile and think of the memories you had with them. You are more at peace with the tragedy that occurred, and you've also accepted that life does need to move on.

Summary

Moving on is not the end goal of grief. All the same, it is never easy, and just like grieving, moving on also takes time. Understanding the roadblocks to overcome destructive patterns in the grieving process is crucial. The bereaved may not be able to see it, but as a close friend, family, or caregiver, you can offer your support and help show them that these emotions that they have held onto aren't helping them to grieve the memory of their beloved.

You must also be wary of all the myths and misconceptions surrounding grief. Knowledge of these fallacies is beneficial for both the bereaved and those wishing to help them. These myths need to be dispelled because it will lead to unhealthy and destructive behaviors.

Chapter 7: How to Comfort Someone Who is Grieving

Grief comes in many shapes and forms, and for many of us, the number one concern when it comes to comforting someone who is grieving is whether or not we are doing or saying the right things. It's understandable and a valid concern. After all, losing someone is not a situation anyone wants to go through very often. It only makes sense that you want to provide the right care to help your grieving friend or relative get through an incredibly dreadful time.

Knowing how to show and express your care and concern can make all the difference in a grieving person's life, and it's often the little things that you do that can genuinely help them come out of their grief and begin to pick up the pieces of their life, to get back to normalcy.

Here are some **Do's** and **Don'ts** to help you on this journey:

The Don'ts

- **Don't assume they want or need space**

Whether this person is your close friend, a neighbor, a colleague, or a family member, they would want to hear from you. Expressing your genuine concern to check to see if they are ok can ease the grief burden they carry in their hearts. The closer you are to a person, the greater the need for you to reach out and offer comfort. Knowing that their closest and dearest friends and family are there for them is something a grieving person needs to help them get through this tough time.

- **Don't put a positive spin on the situation.**

When it comes to death, it can be hard to find the right words to say. More often than not, we think that it helps to keep things light and positive. There is nothing that we can say or do that could make the pain any lesser, especially in the first few days or weeks. Someone is experiencing pain, so avoid phrases such as "They are in a better place," "It was their time," 'It's meant to be," or 'Heaven just received an angel." While these words sound good, we don't know for sure where the deceased person is. What's more, the person grieving doesn't care whether it's meant to be or if their loved one is in a better place. They want them back on earth right now, right by their side.

- **Don't compare your experiences.**

When someone just lost a loved one, the pain is fresh. The memories are fresh, and there's a whole load of emotions going through their mind. The last thing you want to do is tell them about your own experiences. Nobody, least of all the grieving person, wants to hear it. If you have an extremely fitting comparison, then you can open up and share your experience with this person once the dust has settled a little.

- **Don't diminish their feelings.**

If someone is sad, they're sad. It doesn't matter if it's a pet goldfish, their neighbor's grandmother, or step-father. Before you brush them off, just think about how you reacted when your favorite singer or actor died. Everyone around the world grieved, and it probably made you feel comforted knowing you could grieve along with them and that they understood your pain. This is the same feeling someone who is grieving is going through. Their feelings are valid no matter how distant or close they are to the deceased. They may have lost touch with the deceased, but they shared a meaningful connection at some point in their lives. It is not your place to invalidate their feelings, whether or not you understand them.

- **Don't wait to reach out.**

Even if you haven't seen this person in a long time, knowing that they have lost a loved one is all the reason you need to reach out to offer your condolences. Knowing people around them from near and far are sharing their pain helps a person get through their day a little by little. Being there for them is all they need right now.

- **Don't put a timeline on grieve.**

People grieve in different ways. Some grieve silently, some talk about it, some blog about it, some write about it. Some people even make songs about it. Some people even end up overeating or drinking as a way to cope. Some people take a few months, and some take years. Who has the right to tell someone how one should grieve and for how long? There is no rulebook for grief. So don't expect them to 'get over it.' Understand that while it has been a while, the pain is still there, and little memories or situations may trigger their grief. It is entirely normal to feel profoundly sad for one year or many years - we lost a spark that made us happy, and it will be hard to pick up and get back to normalcy. So don't put pressure on someone who is grieving.

The Do's

And now, we come into the things that you can do and should do more often. When it comes to caring and helping a grieving person, empathy and compassion need to be the frontline emotions.

- **Keep in mind their reactions.**

As mentioned at the start of this chapter, everyone grieves differently. Some people may crack jokes and make everyone laugh around them to soften the pain and blow they feel. Some people prefer to be left alone. Some people prefer being around familiar company.

The thing about grief is that it comes in many forms, and it's tough to predict how someone will react. You've reached out, said something kind, offered help, etc. They thank you and tell you they don't want to talk about it anymore and they would rather be left alone. So what do you do? Be sensitive to this change and give them room to go through the changing emotions they feel. As long as you let them know you're a call away or you are available if they need you, you're good. If they change their minds and need someone to talk to, they can be assured they can find a friend in you.

- **Express your love in a way only you can.**

Depending on how close you are with the person grieving, share your care and love the way only you know. Cry with your best friend, hug your grieving brother, make a cup of coffee for your colleague, and sit together in silence, cook meals for your elderly neighbor who just lost their spouse. Purchase pampering products for your friend. Text an acquaintance to see how they are doing, a friendly pat on the shoulder, and a smile. All of these little things done with good intentions are appreciated. Remember not to overdo it and look out for signs that they don't like it, or not very receptive.

- **Listen to them.**

Active listening allows one to make sense of and understand what the person is saying. It doesn't matter if you don't have a solution. That's not what they are looking for. They want to pour out their feelings, and they want someone to hear them out. So whenever they initiate a conversation, make room for their words and don't feel the need to interject. Remember that you are not a therapist, so you may not have the capacity or expertise to deal with various emotions coming your way. So just give them space to express themselves. Sometimes all everyone needs is a listening ear.

- **Empathize with their feelings.**

Acknowledge just how bad the situation is. Let's face it. A dear one died and left a big, gaping hole in their lives. It's going to take time for them to pick up the pieces and start learning to live life without the deceased. Some days will be good, some days will be awful, and some days will be ok. It'll be a rollercoaster ride of emotions. Agreeing with someone that things are bad is a lot more supportive than telling them that 'it could've been worse.'

- **Offer to connect them with people in similar situations.**

After a certain time, when you feel that the person has come back to a certain sense of normalcy, it helps to connect them with someone who has gone through the same situation. Some people may feel isolated and may feel that nobody understands the depth of pain they are going through. Talking to someone who has gone through a similar loss might make them feel a connection. They can also gain support and understanding and even healthy ways of coping. Take note that they can always say no if they don't feel like it but if they are open to it, link them to someone else like this could be hugely helpful.

- **Give little and give often.**

Knowing the world goes on despite the pain you

are going through can feel alienating. Every text sent, emails, calls, postcards, voice notices, video calls are all little ways to reach out and check-in. These voices from the outside are reminders that people around the bereaved care, and it is the technological equivalent of having your handheld through it all.

- **Offer practical assistance.**

For the bereaved, it will take time to readjust their way of life now that the deceased is no longer around. The closer you were to the deceased, the more challenging and the more adjustments you need to make. A sense of loss is evident. You can no longer call them - nobody would answer the phone on the other end. The other side of the bed is empty. No laughing at their jokes. No getting big bear hugs from them. It's going to take a lot to readjust, and sometimes, a helping hand goes a long way. A grieving person may not have the headspace, motivation, or energy to call or ask for help. Or they may feel guilty about receiving the attention or fear burdening people around them. So offer the bereaved practical help. Instead of saying, ‘Let me know if there’s anything I can do”, you can try being specific and say, ‘I’m mowing my lawn today. Would you like yours moved too?”. Or “I’m going to the grocery store. What would you like from there?”. Or “I made lasagna. I can bring some over. Let me know when?”. It helps if you are consistent in your offers of assistance so that the bereaved will know that you are there for as long as it takes.

- **Watch out for signs of depression.**

A grieving person will feel plenty of emotions from anger to confusion, isolation, hurt, anxiety, and even the feeling of being disconnected. Among these emotions, it’s also common to feel depressed, especially in the first few months. This is perfectly normal. However, if signs of depression seem to be constant and taking longer to fade, then this may mean that normal grief has evolved to clinical depression. Some of these signs could be an extreme focus on death, neglecting personal hygiene, substance or alcohol abuse, inability to enjoy life, and difficulty in functioning in daily life.

Keep in mind that this is a hard line to tread on, simply because it is hard to discern whether the person is grieving or depressed. Give them time to grieve but checking up on them as often as you can help you notice whether it is a condition that is different to grieve. When you feel that it could be depression, help them to seek professional help.

- **Offer prayers and encouragement.**

You may not be religious, but the bereaved could be. Or the bereaved is not religious, but you are. Either way, offer up prayers and encouragement to them either in the form of letters, texts, or calls. Keep in mind never to force down your beliefs and never overdo it because it can cause more harm than good. Keep it simple, and keep it light.

How to Avoid Compassion Fatigue?

If you are a caregiver to a person going through grief, this can put you at risk of compassion fatigue.

Compassion fatigue is the side effect of caring for someone in need. If not managed well, compassion fatigue can cause physical and emotional exhaustion to the caregiver, reducing their ability to empathize. It can also reduce your ability to provide the warmth, care, and engagement required to the bereaved.

To protect yourself, it's essential to learn strategies to help you cope. Here are a few:

- **Prioritize self-care.**

Self-care is essential to anyone but more so for

long-term caregivers. Self-care helps you maintain a healthy mental and physical well being. It means taking time out for yourself, even if it is for a few hours a day. It isn't selfish to have a few hours to yourself. It's healthy, and it makes you a better caregiver.

While self-care routines are different for everyone, it usually involves doing something for yourself. Some examples - having your favorite meal, meditation, watching your favorite movie, taking a long bath, having some downtime, or even taking a walk in nature. The idea here is to give yourself some time to focus solely on your needs.

- **Spend time with people outside your caregiver life.**

Whether it's spending time with family or friends, an essential part of maintaining a balanced life is to keep up with social connections. Sometimes you may be too tired for social interactions, but something simple such as sharing a meal, talking on the phone, chatting, and video calls are ways to remove yourself from your caregiver life and worries.

- **Write or paint your thoughts.**

Writing or blogging is a known stress reduction technique. The same goes for coloring or painting. Channeling your thoughts and feelings to the written word or art is a very therapeutic way of getting rid of compassion fatigue.

Summary

Grief is a terrible emotion to feel. When someone is grieving, compassion and patience need to be a champion in helping you, help them. This chapter describes how you can comfort someone who has suffered a loss or is grieving. Listening, offering practical assistance, knowing what to say and not to say are useful things we can learn in helping the bereaved. This chapter also concludes with some simple ways of how a caregiver can prevent compassion burnout or compassion fatigue. More often, the best way to consistently provide better caregiving assistance is to take a break for yourself, which includes self-care and coping strategies for your emotional and mental wealth-being. This can be as simple as enjoying a cup of coffee in the quiet of the morning, a 10-minute meditation, going for a run, or journaling.

Conclusion

Thank you for making it through to the end of *How to Deal with Grief, Loss, and Death.* Let's hope it was informative and able to provide you with all of the tools you need to achieve your goals, whatever they may be.

You will heal. You will move on. You will become stronger despite your pain. It doesn't feel like it right now, but everyone who has ever gone through the process will tell you that it does get better. Losing someone you love will never be an easy process to deal with, but it is not an impossible process to overcome.

Healing begins the moment you stop running away from your pain. Fight the urge to do it because, just like running away from your problems, trying to run away from the pain is never going to help. Identify your emotions and permit yourself to feel them. You don't have to be afraid or feel guilty about any emotion you feel during this time, including anger. Embrace your suffering. There is no need to try and reason or justify them. All you have to do right now is embrace the way that you feel. No matter what emotion you feel, let it all out. Let it pour out of you like a flood if you must. Bottled emotions are never going to do anyone any good. Talk to a friend or family member, scribble in a journal, seek the help of a counselor or therapist if you must. The point is that you need to do whatever it takes to properly process and work through your emotions. The liberating exercise of processing your emotions will eventually give you a sense of relief and perspective as you journey toward the end of your grieving process.

As you work through the stages of grief, remember to be patient with yourself. Grief and loss are an emotional wound that you need to heal from, and just like physical wounds, it will require time to heal properly. Emotional healing is the process that needs to happen gradually and at your own pace. Every person is different. Some people might go through grief stages within the next six months, while others may require a little more time before they start to feel like themselves again. It doesn't matter how much time you require to heal. All that matters is that you *heal*. That can only happen if you allow yourself to take as much time as you need to work through your stages of grief. This is a very painful and traumatizing time you're going through, and the last thing you should be worried about is trying to rush through the process.

Ignore the pressure of trying to get over your grief as quickly as possible. Ignore the advice to "move on" that you will no doubt be hearing multiple times along the way. You don't have to force yourself to do anything that you are not ready for. Your grieving process is unique to your own experience, and no one is ever going to understand just how much pain you're going through. All they can do is say what they think is going to help. There is no simple way to get over your loss quickly, and even with the techniques in this book, it is still going to take time before you feel like your old self again. You will never "get over it" or "move on" from your loved one, and you don't have to either.

The depth of the grief you feel is the price you pay for love. That immense pain you feel is a reflection of how much this person meant to you. It reflects the extent of your love, and you shouldn't have to feel rushed into getting over them. The truth is, you will never completely "get over" them, and they will be a permanent part of your life. You will continue to talk about them for the rest of your life and reminisce on the memories that you shared. This is how they remain a part of your life long after they are gone.

When someone you love is gone forever, guilt is a normal part of the process. You think about all the things you wished you had done or said. You might feel guilty because it may feel as though you didn't love them as much as you should have when they were alive. You think about all the things you would change right now if you could have them back in your life again. If there is one thing you can take away from your grieving process, it is this: *The life you shared with your loved one was perfect the way it was.* They know how much you loved them, even if it feels like you didn't express it as much as you should have. They loved you just as much as you love them, even if it was never said. That is the beauty of human relationships. We understand how the ones we love feel, and we don't need to put it into words all the time. The fact that you continue to think about them years after they are gone is proof of how real the love was.

Your loved one will never truly be gone because they will always be a part of your life for *the rest* of your life. Their body may be gone, but their spirit will live on forever in the memories that you built together. The ones you love will live on forever because they continue to survive in the memories of the people they left behind. That is the legacy of love they left for you. The conversations you had with them will go on forever in your mind, and you will continue to think about them and feel their presence. Through the dilemmas, joys, happiness, and sorrows now and the ones yet to come, the people you love will be by your side in spirit as long as we continue to keep their memory alive in our hearts forever.

Finally, if you found this book useful in any way, a

review on Amazon is always appreciated!

One more thing

If you enjoyed this book and found it helpful, I'd be very grateful if you'd post a short review. Your support does make a difference, and I read all the reviews personally so I can get your feedback and make this book even better. I love hearing from my readers, and I'd really appreciate it if you leave your honest feedback.

Thank you for reading!

References

Chill Out: How to Use Progressive Muscle Relaxation to Quell Anxiety. (n.d.). Verywell Mind. https://www.verywellmind.com/how-do-i-practice-progressive-muscle-relaxation-3024400

Eikenberry, K. (2020, April 29). *The Power of Gratitude*. Success Consciousness. https://www.successconsciousness.com/blog/personal-development/power-of-gratitude/

Harvard Health Publishing. (n.d.). Sour mood getting you down? Get back to nature. Harvard Health.

https://www.health.harvard.edu/mind-and-mood/sour-mood-getting-you-down-get-back-to-nature

G. (n.d.). *Deepak Chopra's 7-Step Exercise to Release Emotional Turbulence*. Gaiam. https://www.gaiam.com/blogs/discover/deepak-chopras-7-step-exercise-to-release-emotional-turbulence

Haley, E. (2020, April 16). *5 Benefits of Grief Journaling*. Whats Your Grief. https://whatsyourgrief.com/5-benefits-of-grief-journaling/

Haley, E. (2020b, June 17). *How to Support a Grieving Family Member or Friend: 6* Principles. Whats Your Grief. https://whatsyourgrief.com/support-grieving-family-member-friend-6-principals/

Is Holotropic Breathwork Right For You? (n.d.). Verywell Mind.

https://www.verywellmind.com/holotropic-breathwork-4175431

Loss, C. F. (2016, December 14). *Nurturing Yourself When You're Grieving*. Center for Loss & Life Transition. https://www.centerforloss.com/2016/12/nurturing-youre-grieving/

Pilz, K. (2020, November 18). *How Journaling Helped Me Heal from Grief and How It Can Help You* Too. Tiny Buddha. https://tinybuddha.com/blog/journaling-process-grief/

Robinson, B. (2019, November 18). The Power Of Gratitude And How It Raises Your Happiness Level. Forbes. https://www.forbes.com/sites/bryanrobinson/2019/11/18/the-power-of-gratitude-and-how-it-raises-your-happiness-level/#3f09ca3e373e

Robinson, L. (n.d.). Relaxation Techniques for Stress Relief - HelpGuide.org. Help Guide.

https://www.helpguide.org/articles/stress/relaxation-techniques-for-stress-relief.htm

Stang, H. (2020, April 19). 9 Self-Care Tips For Grief: Reduce Your Suffering in Mind, Body & Spirit. Mindfulness & Grief: Meditation for Life After Loss. https://mindfulnessandgrief.com/9-self-care-tips-for-grief/

Sterling, J. (2020, November 17). *How to Release Painful Memories & Emotions Stored in Your Body*. Tiny Buddha. https://tinybuddha.com/blog/how-to-release-the-painful-memories-emotions-stored-in-your-body/

Stöppler, M. C. (2012, August 13). *Progressive Muscle Relaxation for Stress and Insomnia*. WebMD. https://www.webmd.com/sleep-disorders/muscle-relaxation-for-stress-insomnia

Tartakovsky, M. M. S. (2018, July 8). *How to Sit with Painful Emotions*. World of Psychology. https://psychcentral.com/blog/how-to-sit-with-painful-emotions/

The Transformative Power of Gratitude. (n.d.). Huffpost. https://www.huffpost.com/entry/the-transformative-power-_2_b_6982152

Understanding grief and loss – for friends and family | headspace. (n.d.). Headspace. https://headspace.org.au/friends-and-family/understanding-grief-and-loss-for-family-and-friends/

Printed in Great Britain
by Amazon

64858456R00099